MY FIRST SPACE ATLAS

Illustrated by Paul Daviz
Written by Jane Wilsher

EARTHAWARE
KIDS

Illustrated by Paul Daviz

Written by Jane Wilsher

Space Consultant – Professor Ben Maughan, University of Bristol

weldon**owen**

Copyright © EarthAware Kids, 2023

Published by EarthAware Kids
Created by Weldon Owen Children's Books
A subsidiary of Insight International, LP.

PO Box 3088
San Rafael, CA 94912
www.insighteditions.com

Weldon Owen Children's Books
Editor: Catherine Ard
Designer: Tory Gordon-Harris
Senior Production Manager: Greg Steffen
Art Director: Stuart Smith
Publisher: Sue Grabham

Insight Editions
Publisher: Raoul Goff

ISBN: 978-1-68188-888-0

Manufactured, printed, and assembled in China
First printing October, 2022

XYP1022

FSC
www.fsc.org
100%
Paper from well-managed forests
FSC® C152346

CONTENTS

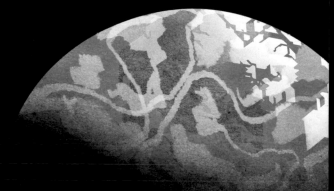

THE NIGHT SKY

Look up! Every night, the sky puts on a dazzling light show. It is hard to believe, but you are staring deep into Space. Each tiny, twinkling light that you see is a distant star or planet. There is the friendly face of the Moon, too. It gazes down on you as you gaze back.

Now think about this as you look up at the night sky. You are standing on a big, round, rocky planet. This is Earth, your home. Earth feels so unbelievably big, but it is just one small planet among billions in this enormous place called Space.

Moon

MOON BUNNY

The Moon has dark patches on its surface. Some people think they look like a rabbit with two long ears. What do you see?

BLAZING FIREBALLS

This light zooming across the sky is a space rock that has come close to Earth. It turns into a ball of fire called a shooting star.

shooting star

WARM BLANKET

Earth has an invisible layer of air that you breathe called the atmosphere. It keeps the Earth nice and warm.

STARGAZING

What can you see in the night sky? In towns and cities, the glow of street lights makes it harder to see the stars.

What can you see in the night sky?

airplane

shooting star

Venus

BRIGHT PLANETS

Some of the brightest lights in the night sky are planets. The most visible one is Venus.

SPOT IT!

How many people are looking at the night sky? Can you see a rocket zooming into Space?

STARRY SKY

On a clear night, you might see a hazy band of light. This is the Milky Way—our own galaxy, which is filled with billions of stars.

International Space Station

MOVING LIGHTS

Astronauts work on the International Space Station, or ISS. Look out for its glimmering lights moving across the sky.

LOOKING CLOSER

People can look at the night sky through a telescope. It makes distant things look bigger and brighter.

telescope

rocket

observatory

SUPER TELESCOPE

Inside an observatory, there is a powerful telescope. The building's domed roof opens up to the stars.

Moon

rocket

Milky Way

planet

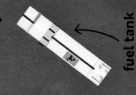

International Space Station

crew capsule

2. Second fuel tank falls away.

fuel tank

3, 2, 1, BLASTOFF!

Imagine you are an astronaut in a rocket launching into Space. The engines roar and the rocket shakes and rattles as it picks up speed. You can hear people talking to you over the radio. They are part of a team of scientists at Mission Control, and they make sure everything goes like clockwork. In just eight minutes, you will leave Earth far behind and enter the blackness of Space.

Spacecraft take off from a huge space center. It takes years to prepare for a rocket launch. Astronauts need to train for life in Space and practice the jobs they will do when they get there.

crew capsule

CREW CAPSULE

The astronauts travel inside a small capsule at the top of the rocket. Only this part of the rocket goes all the way to Space.

fuel tanks

FULL TANKS

A rocket uses lots of fuel to blast into Space. When the fuel tanks are empty, they fall back to Earth.

SPOT IT!
Can you see the crew capsule? Where are the rocket's engines?

1. First fuel tank falls away.

fuel tank

What happens after liftoff?

fuel tanks

BLASTOFF
Powerful engines help lift the rocket into the sky.

engines

BURNING UP
Flames and smoke billow from the rocket's engines.

CHEERING CROWD
Lots of people go to watch the launch. The viewing stand is a safe distance from the rocket.

SHAKING
The rocket makes a rumbling roar as it lifts off. Onlookers can feel the ground shaking under their feet.

LIVING IN SPACE

Ready to dock! Just imagine, you have spent 19 hours in a rocket traveling from Earth. Now it is time to join the International Space Station, or ISS. The ISS moves incredibly quickly, taking just 90 minutes to zoom around our planet. For the next six months, this huge machine will be home.

Astronauts from around the world work, eat, exercise, and sleep here, just like on Earth. The difference is that in Space things are weightless—astronauts and objects float around if they are not held down.

crew capsule

sleeping bag

SWEET DREAMS
Sleeping bags are fixed to the wall. This stops astronauts drifting away when they doze off!

NEW ARRIVALS
When a rocket arrives, it joins onto the International Space Station. This is called docking.

Moon

TOILET TIME
A special toilet sucks away waste and blasts it into Space.

toilet

drink pouch

What does an astronaut do on the ISS?

7 A.M. breakfast   **8 A.M.** exercise   **11 A.M.** experiments

CALLING EARTH

Astronauts use a computer to phone home. They wear a headset to chat to their families.

headset

HOUSTON

LONDON

MOSCOW

Earth

SPOT IT!
What are the plants in the science lab for? How many astronauts can you see?

SPACE GYM

A daily run on a treadmill keeps astronauts fit and strong.

SCIENCE LAB

Astronauts carry out experiments. They study how plants grow in Space.

monitor screen

NO COOKIES!

Crumbly food is not allowed. Crumbs can float into machines and break them.

COMFY CLOTHES

Astronauts do not need to wear spacesuits inside the ISS. They wear normal clothes.

MINTY MOUTHFUL

Toothpaste has to be swallowed. There are no sinks to spit into.

1 P.M. lunch

3 P.M. spacewalk

7 P.M. dinner

9:30 P.M. bedtime

READY FOR A SPACEWALK ?

tether

What do you think it would feel like to go on a spacewalk? You would have to put on a bulky spacesuit and helmet, then open the hatch door and float out into the darkness. Imagine the views of Earth far below!

A special cable, called a tether, keeps astronauts safely attached to the space station while they are outside. There are lots of important jobs to do, such as making repairs, testing equipment, and taking photos. Say, 'Cheese!'

mechanical arm

SUNNY SPACE
Huge solar panels collect energy from the Sun and turn it into electricty for use on the space station.

HELMET CHAT
There's a radio inside the helmet to speak with the crew.

THE EARTH LOOKS BLUE!

International Space Station (ISS)

solar panels

wrist mirror

WARM HANDS
Thick gloves are heated at the fingertips.

Earth

Can you find these things astronauts use?

camera

wrist mirror

tether

visor

HANDY PACK

This backpack provides air and drinking water. It also has jet thrusters, which can zoom the astronaut back to the space station.

BRIGHT LIGHT

A shiny gold visor protects the eyes from the Sun.

SPOT IT!

What are the astronauts wearing on their hands?

Which astronaut has blue stripes on their spacesuit?

SUPER SNAPS

Astronauts send photos of the repairs they make back to Earth.

camera

BENDY SUIT

A spacesuit has fourteen layers. It is shaped in segments, like a caterpillar, so the astronaut can move easily.

WHO'S WHO?

You can tell the astronauts apart by the different-colored stripes on their spacesuits.

astronaut

gloves

A TRIP TO THE MOON

Shut your eyes and imagine you are on the Moon, bumping along in a moon buggy. Watch out for the holes! This special car is called a lunar rover. There are no sides or roof, just seats, wheels, and a floor. It can fold up to fit inside a rocket.

Look! There is our beautiful blue and green planet in the distance. From the Moon, you can see Earth's land, its oceans, and the clouds drifting across it. The Moon is very different. There are no trees or water, but there is still plenty to explore. You can collect moon rocks and take pictures of everything you see.

Earth

LASTING PRINTS

Tracks made in the dusty surface stay forever. There is no wind or rain to wear them away.

footprints

lunar rover

Have you noticed how the Moon's shape seems to change in the night sky?

crescent moon

first quarter

MOON MOVIE

Can you see the camera? Its pictures are sent back to Earth by the antenna.

antenna

camera

SPOT IT!
Can you find the footprints in the dust? How many wheels does the lunar rover have?

TOUGH TIRES

Special metal wheels stop the lunar rover from sinking into the soft, dusty ground.

LUNAR LANDSCAPE

The Moon has mountains and valleys and wide, flat areas.

crater

HUGE HOLES

Bowl-shaped holes called craters cover the surface. They were made by giant space rocks that crashed into the Moon.

full moon

last quarter

oUR VERY oWN STAR

What do you think this giant ball of fire might be? It is our star in Space—the Sun! It is hard to believe, but the sunshine that warms your face on a summer's day and peeps through the curtains every morning comes from this huge, superhot star. The Sun's rays travel millions of miles through Space to reach us. Everything that lives on Earth needs the Sun to survive. It gives us heat and light and helps plants to grow.

Astronauts cannot visit the Sun, because it is much too hot and too far way. Instead, we send spacecraft with no people on board called probes. They gather information and send it back to Earth, where scientists examine the findings.

HOW HOT?
The surface of the Sun is five times hotter than any volcano erupting on Earth.

SCORCHING CORONA
The corona is a layer of glowing gases that surrounds the Sun. It is 100 times hotter than the Sun's surface.

SPOT THE DOTS
Darker patches on the Sun are called sunspots. They are cooler than other parts of the surface.

What does the Sun give us?   light

BIG EXPLOSIONS!

The bright flashes on the Sun's surface are called solar flares. They sometimes shoot hot material into Space.

solar flare

SPOT IT!

Can you see the solar panels on the space probe?

How many solar flares can you see?

heat shield

HOT WORK

A special shield protects the probe from the Sun's heat.

HOW BIG?

If the Sun was hollow, more than a million Earths could fit inside it.

space probe

solar panel

SPACE SPY

A probe circles around the Sun and studies it close up.

DON'T LOOK!

Never look directly at the Sun. It can burn your eyes.

sunshine for plants

warmth

energy

15

ROCK BAND

Asteroids are lumps of space rock. There are nearly two million of them floating in a band called the asteroid belt.

asteroid belt

Venus

SPACE GIANT

Jupiter is the largest planet in the Solar System.

Jupiter

TOO COLD

Planets that are furthest from the Sun are freezing cold.

Neptune

KNOCKED OVER

Scientists think a giant rock may have crashed into Uranus. Now it is tipped on its side.

Uranus

MEET THE NEIGHBORS

If you were able to zoom far out into Space and look around, you would see the Solar System—our neighborhood in Space. Right in the middle is the fiery Sun. Moving around the Sun, there are eight giant planets, including Earth. Can you find our planet? There are millions of big and small rocks, too.

In Space, everything is always on the move. The planets travel around the Sun in loops called orbits. They also spin nonstop. You cannot feel it, but Earth is spinning at 1,000 miles per hour as you read this!

What is in the Solar System?

 Sun **planets** **dwarf planets**   **moons**

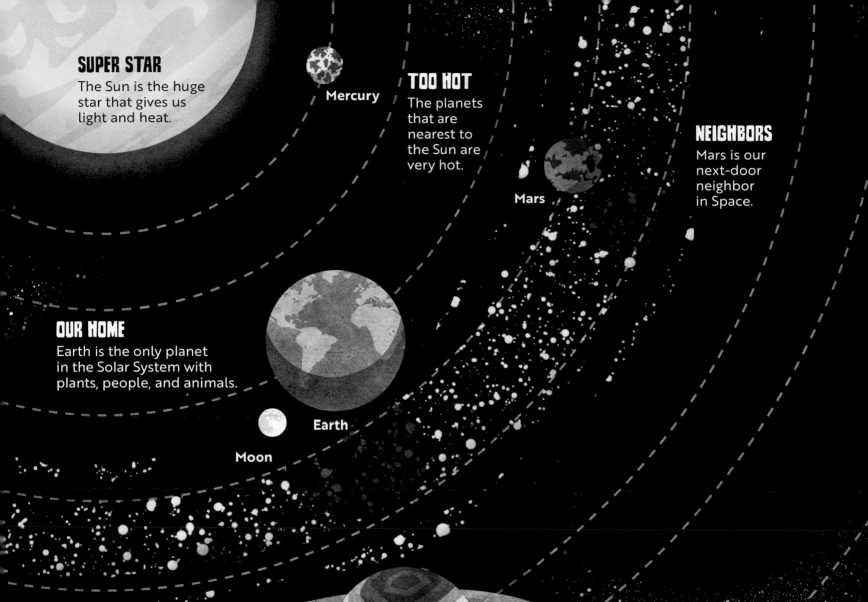

SUPER STAR
The Sun is the huge star that gives us light and heat.

Mercury

TOO HOT
The planets that are nearest to the Sun are very hot.

NEIGHBORS
Mars is our next-door neighbor in Space.

Mars

OUR HOME
Earth is the only planet in the Solar System with plants, people, and animals.

Earth

Moon

ROCKY RINGS
Lumps of ice and rock make rings around Saturn. Some pieces are tiny. Others are as big as a house.

Saturn

LITTLE ONES
There are five dwarf planets in the Solar System. They are too small to be real planets. Pluto is the largest of them.

Pluto

LOOPY LAPS
The blue lines show the routes that the planets take around the Sun.

SPOT IT!
Can you see a planet with a red spot?

How many planets have rings around them?

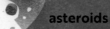

comets · asteroids · meteoroids · meteors

WHO LIVES ON MARS?

Do you know what this roaming robot is doing? It is a Mars rover on a mission to explore our nearest neighbor in Space. So far, no humans have set foot on this rocky red planet. Probes and rovers controlled by people on Earth are sent to discover more about Mars. The rovers carry special tools and science equipment to search for signs of life. Scientists want to know whether people could live here one day.

Would you like to visit Mars? Although it is the closest planet to Earth, it is millions of miles away. It would take about nine months on board a speeding rocket to get there!

Deimos

ROVING EXPLORER

A rover spends years exploring and sending pictures and information back to Earth.

camera

Mars rover

BUMPY RIDE

Six springy wheels help the rover roll over knee-high rocks.

wheels

TWO MOONS

Mars has two moons. One is called Phobos and the other is called Deimos. They are both much smaller than Earth's moon.

Phobos

SPOT IT!

How many moons can you see?

Can you see a camera that sends pictures back to Earth?

ROCKY LANDSCAPE

Mars has tall mountains, huge volcanoes, and deep valleys. So far, the only water the rovers have found is ice.

Mars helicopter

HANDY ARM

The end of the robotic arm can hold tools for collecting and testing rocks.

HIGH FLYER

A little helicopter gives a bird's eye view of the landscape and can land in places that a rover cannot reach.

robotic arm

SPACE GARDENING

Scientists believe that peas, carrots, and other vegetables could be grown in the soil on Mars.

How do rovers land?

1. Parachute goes up!

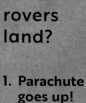

rover capsule

2. Rover detaches.

folded rover

3. Jets on!

jets

4. Rover unfolds . . .

. . . and is ready to explore!

Earth

satellite

LOOK OUT!
Scientists on Earth send radio waves into Space to track lumps of junk so that space missions can keep clear.

beam of radio waves

SPACE JUNK

Watch out! In Space, you will need to dodge space junk and avoid flying litter. Bolts, screws, astronauts' tools, and bits of old rockets are just some of the things that you could see whizzing past on their route around Earth.

All this junk has come from our planet. We need to clean up Space to make it safe for future missions. Even tiny objects are dangerous when they are speeding along at 17,000 miles per hour!

Can you spot this space junk?  camera pliers screw

STAY CLEAR!

The International Space Station has to move its position if there is space junk in its path.

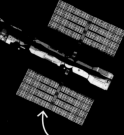

International Space Station

SPOT IT!

How many dropped astronauts' gloves can you see?

Can you see the beam of radio waves?

BROKEN MACHINES

There are thousands of communication machines called satellites in Space. When they break, they are stuck there.

broken satellite

SPEEDY PAINT

Tiny paint flecks from rockets cause serious damage if they crash into spacecraft at high speeds.

WHOOPS!

Cameras, gloves, and other objects were dropped by astronauts on spacewalks.

YELLOW ICE

Astronauts' pee is dumped into Space and freezes into crystals.

toothbrush   bolt   wrist mirror   spatula

MERCURY
This is THE place to spend your birthday. One day on Mercury lasts for 58 Earth days!

VENUS
Yuk! This planet smells of bad eggs! It is boiling hot and there are fiery volcanoes and acid rain.

Sun

Mercury

Venus

Earth

Mars

Asteroid belt

POSTCARDS FROM THE PLANETS

What would you discover if you could whiz off into the Solar System? After visiting each of the eight planets, you would have very different adventures to write about on your postcards home.

Some planets are boiling hot and some are freezing cold. The planets are a rainbow of colors because they are made from different rocks and gases. Mercury, Venus, Earth, and Mars are dry and rocky. Jupiter, Saturn, Uranus, and Neptune are balls of swirling gas. If you tried to land on the gas planets, you would fall straight through!

SATURN
Wish you were here! The views on Saturn are out of this world. Seven rings made from chunks of ice and rock sparkle in the sky. I have counted more than 80 moons so far ...

What are the planets in the Solar System?

Sun

Mercury

Venus

Earth

MARS

Spending a few days on this dusty, rocky planet. There are huge dust storms that last for weeks on end. In fact, the wind is picking up right now. Yikes!

SPOT IT!
How many blue planets can you see?

Which is the red planet?

JUPITER

Greetings from this giant gas planet. The weather is bad! A storm three times bigger than Earth has been raging here for hundreds of years.

Jupiter

Saturn

URANUS

This planet is icy, smelly, and covered in a slushy ocean. The wind is full of ice crystals, too. Brrrrrr!

Uranus

NEPTUNE

This stop is over two billion miles from Earth. It reminds me of Uranus, because it is very cold and icy. There is thick fog and the wind never stops blowing.

Neptune

Mars

Jupiter

Saturn

Uranus

Neptune

WELCOME TO THE MILKY WAY!

Imagine a place so gigantic that it would take a rocket millions of years to fly from one side to the other. You live inside that place—it is a galaxy! A galaxy is a huge collection of gas, dust, and billions of stars and planets. Planet Earth and everything in the Solar System are in a swirly galaxy called the Milky Way.

On a clear night, when you look up at the sky you see thousands of higgledy-piggledy stars splattered like paint. This is not the whole of Space that you see, but just the stars in our little corner of the Milky Way.

HOW FAR?

After the Sun, the next nearest star to Earth is 24 trillion miles away! It is called Proxima Centauri.

HUNGRY HOLE

There is a supermassive black hole hidden at the center of our galaxy! Black holes suck in anything that comes too close.

spiral arm

LONG ARMS

The Milky Way is a spiral shape with four long, curving arms.

YOU ARE HERE

What is in the Milky Way?   clouds of dust   thousands of nebulas   millions of black holes

SPILT MILK

Can you guess how the Milky Way got its name? From Earth the stars look like tiny drops of milk splashed across the sky.

ANYIONE THERE?

Our galaxy has billions of planets and moons that move around stars like our Sun. Scientists study them for signs of life.

SPOT IT!

Where can you find the supermassive black hole?

Can you see a nebula?

single star

bright stars

STAR BABIES

The glowing colored lights are giant clouds of dust and gas called nebulas. They are where new stars are born.

nebula

hundreds of billions of planets

hundreds of billions of moons

hundreds of billions of stars

THE UNIVERSE

What would you see if you could zoom to the far reaches of Outer Space? You would find an inky blackness peppered with 100 billion glowing galaxies, each one packed with billions of stars. All of the galaxies and absolutely everything in Space is called the Universe. The Earth and the Sun are just tiny pinpricks inside one galaxy called the Milky Way.

The Universe is more enormous than anyone can imagine! It stretches further than the most powerful telescope can see. Scientists think that the Universe is still growing and getting bigger every day! There is so much left to discover. Where would you like to explore?

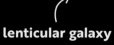

lenticular galaxy

YOU ARE HERE

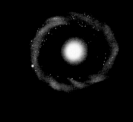

Milky Way

MYSTERIOUS MATTER

Most of the Universe is made up of invisible stuff called dark matter. Scientists know it exists because it pulls and bends things nearby.

OUR NEIGHBORHOOD

Andromeda is the nearest large galaxy to the Milky Way. It can sometimes be seen from Earth as a bright smudge in the night sky.

irregular galaxy

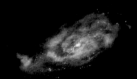

Andromeda

far-off galaxy

FAR AND AWAY

The most distant galaxies look like faint red smudges, even when using the biggest telescopes.

What are the different galaxy shapes?

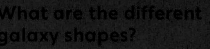
elliptical

spiral

SPOT IT!
Can you see a black hole?

How many spiral galaxies can you spot?

HOW BIG?
Each one of these glowing specks is a galaxy filled with billions of stars.

spiral galaxy

elliptical galaxy

GALAXY SHAPES
Galaxies come in different shapes. Many are spirals, but they can also look like hats, balls, eggs, or strange blobs.

black hole

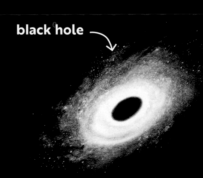

BLACK HOLES
When a very big star dies, it explodes and turns into a black hole. Black holes suck in everything around them—even stars.

lenticular

irregular

LOOKING UP AT SPACE

You can be a space explorer without ever leaving planet Earth. Space scientists study the Moon, stars, and planets using powerful telescopes that show faraway things up close.

There are different kinds of telescope. A radio telescope looks like a huge bowl. It picks up invisible radio waves and shows us things we can't see with our eyes. Another type of telescope sits inside a domed building called an observatory. The roof opens and the telescope points upward to the glittering night sky above. The best views of all come from space telescopes. These powerful machines are launched into Space by rockets. They send pictures and information back to Earth.

radio telescope

TUNE IN
Radio telescopes pick up energy from invisible things, such as black holes.

DAY AND NIGHT
A radio telescope receives information 24 hours a day.

What do we use to study Space?   binoculars   telescope

Venus

crescent moon

SPACE SPIES
Thousands of miles above Earth, space telescopes look far out into the Universe.

SPOT IT!
Can you see the planet Venus in the night sky?
Which telescope looks like a bowl?

opening for telescope

observatory

MOVE IT
The telescope can swivel and point in different directions. This allows it to see the whole sky.

telescope

BIG TELESCOPE
Telescopes detect light from stars, planets, and galaxies. They work best on cloudless nights.

STARGAZERS
Often, an observatory allows visitors to take a look at the telescope.

radio telescope

observatory

James Webb space telescope

SPACE WORDS

ANTENNA—a machine that sends and receives radio signals.

ASTEROID—an oddly shaped rock that travels around the Sun in Space. Some asteroids are the size of a car, and others are hundreds of miles wide.

ASTEROID BELT—a band of nearly two million space rocks, or asteroids, surrounding the Sun.

ASTRONAUT—a person who travels into Space.

ATMOSPHERE—an invisible layer of gases that surrounds a planet, moon, or star.

BLACK HOLE—a huge place in Space, created when a big star explodes. Nothing can escape from a black hole – including light.

CAPSULE—the top part of a rocket that goes all the way to Space.

COMET—a large object with a long tail, made from dust and ice.

CRATER—a large, bowl-shaped dip in the ground, caused by a space rock, or meteorite.

DOCK—when a rocket capsule attaches to the International Space Station.

DWARF PLANET—an object too small to be a proper planet. Scientists have named five in our Solar System, including Pluto.

GALAXY—a huge collection of stars, planets, gas and dust. Galaxies come in many different shapes and can have billions of stars in them. Our galaxy is called the Milky Way.

HATCH—a door in a spacecraft.

METEOR—a fast-traveling space rock that burns up in the atmosphere. It is also called a shooting star.

METEORITE—a small space rock that collides with a planet.

METEOROID—a piece of space rock that has broken off from an asteroid or comet. Meteoroids can be as small as a grain of sand or as big as a car.

MISSION CONTROL—a team of space experts on Earth. They make sure that space travel and life on the International Space Station runs smoothly.

MOON—an object that travels around a planet or asteroid. Earth has one moon, Mars has two moons, and Saturn has more than 80.

NEBULA—a giant cloud of dust or gas in Space.

OBSERVATORY—a building containing a powerful telescope for looking into Space.

ORBIT—the curved path a planet, satellite, or spacecraft takes as it

PROBE—a spacecraft without any people on board.

ROCKET—a vehicle used for traveling into Space.

ROVER—a vehicle without doors or a roof for exploring the surface of a planet or a moon.

SATELLITE—any object that travels around another object in Space. This can be a communication machine circling Earth or a spacecraft zooming around another planet.

SHOOTING STAR—a space rock that moves very quickly through the sky, burning up when it comes close to Earth. It is also called a meteor.

SOLAR PANEL—a piece of equipment that captures sunlight and turns it into electricity.

SOLAR SYSTEM—the eight planets, including Earth, and the dwarf planets, moons, asteroids,

STAR—a ball of gas that shines in the sky. Earth's star is the Sun.

SUN—the star at the center of the Solar System. Its heat and light allow plants, humans, and animals to live on Earth.

TELESCOPE— an instrument used to see things that are very far away. They can be based on Earth or sent into Outer Space.

UNIVERSE—all of Space and everything that has ever existed in it—planets, stars, galaxies, energy, and time.

INDEX